Volcanoes

Copyright © 1988, Raintree Publishers Inc.

Translated by Hess-Inglin Translation Services

Library of Congress Number: 87-28785

1 2 3 4 5 6 7 8 9 0   91 90 89 88 87

Printed and bound in the United States of America.

Library of Congress Cataloging in Publication Data

Volcanoes.

  (Science and its secrets)
  Includes index.
  Summary: Presents a variety of facts about volcanoes.
  1. Volcanoes—Juvenile literature. [1. Volcanoes]
I. Series
QE521.3.V64   1988   551.2′1   87-28785
ISBN 0-8172-3081-5 (lib. bdg.)
ISBN 0-8172-3098-X (softcover)

VOLCANOES

Raintree Publishers — Milwaukee

Contents

Location of the World's
Principal Active Volcanoes

What is a volcano?

A cross section of a volcano shows that it is made of three main parts. These are the magma reservoir (or storage chamber), the chimney, and the volcanic form at the earth's surface. But a volcano can have several reservoirs and often has many chimneys.

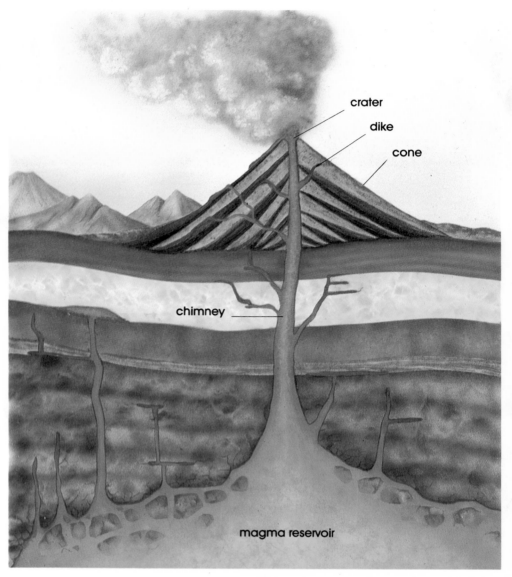

crater
dike
cone
chimney
magma reservoir

Necks and dikes

When a volcano is no longer active, rain, wind, and ice erode its ash cone. The hardened chimney of the volcano then appears. This is called a neck. The famous rock, St. Michel d'Aiguille, in France, is about 269 feet (82 meters) high, and the Devil's Tower, in the United States (Wyoming), is about 865 feet (264 meters) high. These are two very beautiful examples of this. Often, long cracks called fissures, filled with hardened magma are also cleared by erosion. These form great walls, called dikes.

For a long time people believed that a volcano was a mountain which spit flames and streams of fire. In volcanoes, there is no fire, only rocks that have been melted by the earth's heat. These "molten" rocks glow a fiery orange. They are very, very hot, but they are not on fire.

A volcano is made of three parts. These include: a reservoir (or storage chamber), a chimney, and the volcanic form (the part you can see), above the ground. In the earth, miles below the surface, there is a very big cave. This is the reservoir. It is filled with magma, which is hot melted rocks full of gas under pressure. It is, in a sense, the volcano's "stomach." One or several chimneys allow the magma to rise to the surface where it goes out through the volcano's mouth. Once magma has escaped to the earth's surface, it is called lava.

It is then that the outer part of the volcano forms. This is the part you can see. Different types of volcanoes have different forms. Depending on the type, a volcano may have: craters, cones, domes, flows, or ash deposits.

Why are there volcanoes?

Mine workers know that the farther you go down into the earth, the hotter it becomes. On an average, the temperature increases 86°Fahrenheit (30°Celsius) for each mile you descend. At a depth of 22 miles (35 kilometers), the temperature is about 1,832°F (1,000°C). At this temperature, the rocks start to melt and form magma.

The earth is actually a huge, partially melted ball. People are protected from the heat inside by a thin, hardened layer. This layer is called the crust. This crust is only 19 to 43 miles (30 to 70 km) thick. This is not very thick when compared to the earth's 7,899 mile (12,713 km) diameter. Diameter is the distance through the center of an object.

This crust is fissured, or cracked, in many places. Through these cracks, the melted rocks and the trapped gas can escape. At the earth's surface, they build volcanoes. Volcanoes are like the safety valves on pressure cookers that release excess steam. Volcanoes release pressure by allowing excess magma to escape from the planet's depths.

The lava lake of Nyiragongo in Zaïre emptied suddenly in 1977. During the summer of 1982, it filled up again. Molten rock poured into the crater, filling it halfway. Big bubbles caused by rising gas churned the lake's surface. All this lava came from the volcano's reservoir. It reached the surface through fissures in the earth's crust.

The earth: a gigantic nuclear station.

Most of the earth's heat comes from the billions of small radioactive particles in the rocks. These particles give off huge amounts of energy which heat the planet's inside. The earth is like a gigantic nuclear station which has been active for 4.5 billion years. It will stop only in several billion more years. The planet will then be dead, hard and cold all the way to its center. Volcanic explosions, called eruptions, will also stop then.

What is inside the earth?

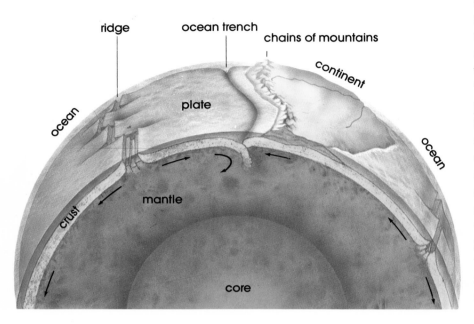

ridge ocean trench chains of mountains continent

ocean plate ocean

crust mantle

core

If the earth could be cut in half, you would see that it is much like a peach. Like a peach, the earth has a pit, called the core. The earth's mantle is like the flesh of the peach. Finally, where the peach has skin, the earth has a crust. The earth's crust is cut into a dozen pieces by long fissures. They line the globe like the seams of a tennis ball (far above).

The Piton de la Fournaise is a volcano on Réunion Island in the Indian Ocean. It often has eruptions. Its basalt lava flows reach temperatures of more than 2012°F (1,100°C). They are among the most fluid and the most rapid in the world (above).

The earth is like a peach, with its skin, its flesh, and its pit. Between the surface and 43 miles (70 km) deep is the skin of the planet. This is the earth's crust. It is hard and has a temperature from 0 to 2,732°F (1,500°C). It is mainly made of a very common volcanic rock: basalt. The crust is broken into a dozen pieces called plates. These plates float. At the edge of the plates, the crust is split by deep fissures. Most of the volcanoes and the centers of earthquakes are found here. The continents on which people live are caught in the plates like pieces of wood frozen in ice. The plates are mainly made of granite, a white rock that shines with many crystals. Granite is often used to make curbing and monuments.

The "flesh" of the planet is the mantle. It is found from 434 to 1,736 miles (700 to 2,800 km) down. Its temperature varies between 2,732° and 4,532°F (1,500° to 2,500°C). The pressure is very great. As far down as 186 miles (300 km), the mantle is made of soft, melted basalt. Below this, the mantle is hard. The soft basalt moves slowly, pushing the plates of the crust floating above. The moving plates shift the continents. They move toward or away from each other very slowly. They move only a few inches per year. This movement is called "continental drift."

The earth's core can be found at depths of 1,736 to 3,949 miles (2,800 to 6,370 km). The core is soft outside and hard in the center. It is composed of iron, nickel, and sulphur. Its temperature ranges from 6,332° to 9,032°F (3,500° to 5,000° C) and the pressure is great.

How is a volcano formed?

Everything starts in the magma reservoir. As magma and the gases that are part of it mix, the pressure in the chamber becomes enormous. The magma tries to escape. It rises, melting gaps, or fissures, in the hard rocks which surround it.

When the magma finally reaches the chimney exit, it explodes. The eruption starts. It is like opening a bottle of soda that has been shaken. The gas bubbles are no longer compressed by the weight of the magma. They expand, suddenly becoming one hundred to two hundred times larger. Then the magma breaks violently into blocks, small stones, and dust, all of which are thrown into the air. Falling back to earth, they form the volcanic cone, with its crater center.

After a lot of gas has escaped, the volcano calms down. The lava then spreads out in great streams, or flows. The eruption totally stops when the magma reservoir is empty or when the volcano loses pressure. Without pressure from below, the magma cannot rise.

Often, the magma in the reservoir is so thick it is almost solid. Thick lava does not flow well. When this happens, two things are possible. First, the magma may ooze slowly out of the volcano. It then forms a lava dome over the volcano. Or, the thick lava may act like a plug and hold the gas beneath it. In this case, the pressure keeps building. The force of the gas soon grows stronger than the lava. Suddenly, the volcano erupts violently. When this happens, the rocks explode, forming a thin powder. This powder buries everything in a wide surrounding area.

In November 1975, a mouth opened in the crater of the volcano Piton de la Fournaise. The lava fell close to the mouth, piling up around it. In a week, the lava built a volcanic cone 131 feet (40 m) high. Each eruption builds one or several such hills. The hills add to the already massive volcano of the Fournaise.

11

When is a volcano extinct?

Is Vesuvius extinct?

Certainly not. Italy's famous Vesuvius was last active in 1944. Two villages and the cableway were destroyed by its ash fallout and lava flow. Vesuvius has been dormant, or inactive, since that year. But what is forty years in the life of a volcano?

Heimaey Island in southern Iceland has several volcanoes. The last to form was Helgafell. It appeared five thousand years ago. Suddenly, on January 23, 1973, a mile-long fissure opened near Helgafell. Fountains of lava spewed 492 feet (150 m) into the air.

Like a human being, a volcano is born, lives, sleeps, awakens, is active, rests, grows old, and finishes by dying. But its life, contrary to a person's, generally lasts thousands or even millions of years. It often lasts so long that volcanologists (people who study volcanoes) have difficulty deciding exactly when it is really extinguished. Because even when dying, a volcano can have one last convulsion.

The famous volcano, Vesuvius, in Italy was dormant almost a thousand years before it suddenly awoke in 79 A.D. and buried the towns of Pompeii and Herculaneum. Before this disaster, everyone considered it a very ordinary mountain, covered with trees and wild vineyards.

Another volcano, Helgafell, in Iceland slept for five thousand years. It suddenly erupted in 1973, just 492 feet (150 m) from a village

The enormous eruptions of Katmai in Alaska in 1912, of Bezymianny in Russia in 1956, and of Arenal in Costa Rica in 1968 surprised many volcanologists. They thought that these three volcanoes were extinct. No one even imagined that Mount Lamington in New Guinea was a volcano. It suddenly erupted in 1951, killing three thousand people.

Today, few volcanologists would be surprised by the awakening of Mount Pelée in Martinique. That volcano has been dormant for fifty years. The same is true of the volcanic cones of the Puys, in the French Massif Central. There the most recent eruption was 3,500 years ago.

12

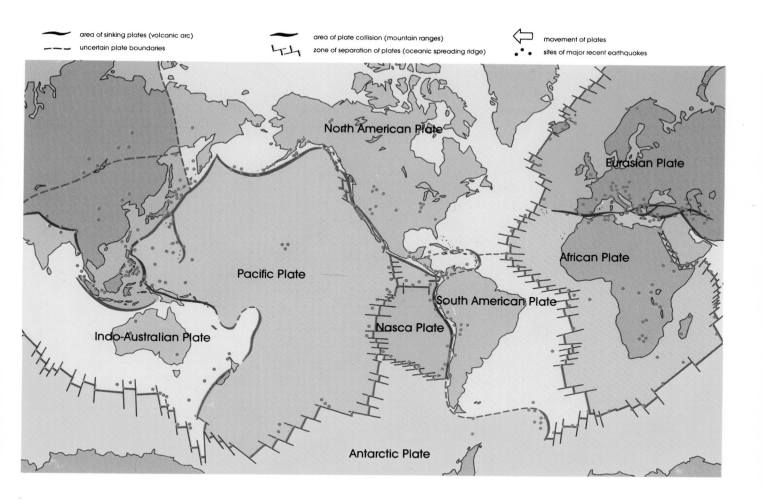

North American Plate

Eurasian Plate

African Plate

Pacific Plate

South American Plate

Nasca Plate

Indo-Australian Plate

Antarctic Plate

Can volcanoes appear anywhere?

Whether you are at the top of the Himalayas, in the fields of France, or in the depths of the Pacific Ocean, you are less than 43 miles (70 km) away from the molten rocks below the earth's crust. If a fissure were to open at that spot, the lava would gush forth to the surface. Thus you can imagine that a volcano could one day form in the middle of places like Paris or New York City.

Actually, it won't happen. The earth is fissured along narrow lines. These lines divide the earth's crust into a dozen plates. Most volcanoes, (almost ninety-five percent), are grouped along these lines. There

the plates either touch or pull away from each other, often making large holes or chipping each other. Neither Paris nor New York City are located on such fissures. But Mexico City, Tokyo, San Francisco, and other large cities in the world are. There, earthquakes are common, and volcanic eruptions are possible.

But some volcanoes are not on the plates' edges. These volcanoes are at their centers. This is true of the volcanic islands of Hawaii. It is also true of the volcanoes of Hoggar in the heart of Africa. These formed over weaknesses in the earth's crust.

The earth's crust is divided into a dozen plates. These float on the deep magma and move about one another. Some plates, like those in the middle of the Atlantic Ocean, move away from each other. Others hit each other and overlap. One then sinks under the other, creating mountain ranges like those around the Pacific Ocean. Most of the great earthquakes occur at the plates' edges.

Are there active volcanoes beneath the sea?

Volcanic activity is much more common beneath the oceans than on land. The rocky ocean bottom, which makes up sixty percent of the earth's surface, is formed of basalt. Each year, many underwater volcanoes erupt, adding more lava. On the bottom of the Pacific Ocean, oceanographers have noted around ten thousand volcanoes that are more than 3,281 feet (1,000 m) high. Several are considered active.

But why doesn't the water in the sea extinguish, or put out, these volcanoes? Because a volcanic eruption is not a fire. The water does cool down the surface of the molten lava. But this only creates a partially hardened carapace, or covering, over it. The inside stays hot.

Some volcanoes are found more than 4,921 feet (1,500 m) under water. These volcanoes have peace-

Some lava flows spread underneath water. They usually take the shape of pillows and are called pillow lava. Many sea bottoms are covered with them. This pillow lava at La Palma in the Canary Islands is above sea level today. The ground on the island has risen since its formation.

ful eruptions. The weight of the water upon them prevents violent explosions. Instead, they just release large lava flows into the water. These twist into many "pillows."

But volcanoes close to the surface are often explosive. In this case, as the sea water comes in contact with the molten rock, it is instantly turned into a huge mass of steam.

No one has yet seen an eruption at a great depth. But oceanographers using deep-sea exploration vessels have gone to the bottom of the Atlantic and Pacific oceans. There they studied recent volcanic forms such as: pillow-shaped and cord-shaped lava flows, lakes of lava, and even huge volcano chimneys.

Devil's Island, Ginni Koma, is a small volcano of the Republic of Djibouti. It began rising beneath the sea ten thousand years ago. That is why it has a haystack shape. Over time, the ground has risen greatly at this place. Today the volcano has completely emerged.

Can volcanoes rise out of the ocean?

Each year, volcanoes rise out of the ocean. Like whales coming to the surface, volcanoes suddenly appear. This is a rare, amazing sight to see.

When water comes in contact with the burning lava, it starts a terrible battle. The sea enters the lava crater, setting off powerful explosions. It then begins spouting clouds of black ash, and creating huge, sometimes very destructive, waves. As the crater closes, it shuts itself off from the ocean. It leaves behind a lake of lava, which dances upon the water, throwing out a shower of orange molten rock.

If the ocean's forces are stronger, the new island disappears. But if the eruption starts again, or if the volcano is stronger, a new island appears.

In 1877, a ship spotted steam escaping from the sea near the islands of Tonga in the south Pacific Ocean. Eight years later, a volcano, the Falcon, appeared at this place. In 1889, another ship planted an English flag on it. But eleven months later, the Falcon disappeared. The waves had worn it away, completely erasing it from the map. In 1892, the volcano erupted again. It surfaced long enough for French sailors to raise the flag, then it sank again.

Two years later, hearing that the Falcon was visible again, the government of Tonga claimed it. But it was all for nothing. The island sank again a few years after. It appeared again in 1900 and sank in 1913. It erupted again between 1921 and 1949, and later in 1970. Today no one bothers planting a flag, as this volcano continues to play hide and seek with the water's surface.

In 1952, the Myozin Syo volcano in southern Japan imitated Falcon Island. But during one terrible explosion, the volcano destroyed the boat carrying scientists who had come to study it. It killed twenty-nine people.

Are there volcanoes under glaciers and lakes?

Volcanoes are often high mountains. So their peaks are covered with snow and ice. In Iceland, the Katla and Grimsvôtn volcanoes are trapped under glaciers. When they erupt, the ice melts. Masses of water, ash, and mud flow down their slopes, destroying everything in their path. In 1918, Katla melted several cubic miles of ice. This formed a river of mud with as much force as the mouth of the powerful Amazon River.

In 1877, the eruption of Cotopaxi in Ecuador also created a river of mud. Flowing at a speed of 31 miles (50 km) an hour, the mass reached a village 149 miles (240 km) away.

These rivers can also form when active craters have lakes. In 1919, the crater lake of Kelut in Indonesia exploded violently and overflowed. Hot mud torrents, or streams, filled the valleys around the volcano in forty-five minutes. One hundred villages were destroyed and five thousand people died.

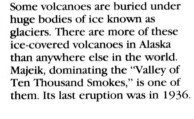

Some volcanoes are buried under huge bodies of ice known as glaciers. There are more of these ice-covered volcanoes in Alaska than anywhere else in the world. Majeik, dominating the "Valley of Ten Thousand Smokes," is one of them. Its last eruption was in 1936.

The year 1980 marks the eruption of Mount St. Helens in the United States (Washington State). A huge avalanche of rocks made Spirit Lake, north of the volcano, overflow. Huge rivers of mud poured down into the valleys. The rivers destroyed 250 houses, seven bridges, 37 miles (60 km) of road, and a train. Sometimes, heavy rains or steam gathering in the ash clouds are enough to collapse entire sections of a weak volcanic cone. A monstrous landslide on the Unzendake Volcano in Japan in 1792 is an example of this. It carried off ten thousand people, then drowned five thousand more. The mass of soil finally ended its course in the sea. There it created a gigantic wave.

In two thousand years, rivers of volcanic mud have killed thirty thousand people. During the same period, lava flows have killed two thousand.

How many active volcanoes are there in the world?

Volcanologists say a volcano is active if there has been even one eruption in recorded history. Today there are five hundred known active volcanoes. Three hundred of these are in and around the Pacific Ocean. But this number only includes those above sea level. The oceanic volcanoes are much more numerous. However, they are very difficult to study.

But if all the recent volcanoes found on the continents are counted —extinct or not—they number about ten thousand. There are more than three times that number in the ocean depths.

Thanks to historical documents and to recent studies, experts have made a list of the almost six thousand volcanic activities on the earth. On an average, there are twenty eruptions per year above sea level.

Do volcanoes occur in clusters?

Volcanoes seem to occur in clusters. In France, more than one thousand volcanoes are found in the Massif Central. The oldest were formed 25 million years ago. The youngest is the crater lake called Pavin. It appeared 3,500 years ago.

Newspapers, radio, and television mention volcanoes only when they threaten human lives, which is rare. They ignore the eruptions which shake the earth's unoccupied places. There are many each year. Some of these eruptions happen at Anak Krakatoa. This volcano is often active. It throws its plumes of ash every few minutes. On its deserted island in the middle of the Sunda Strait, the volcano is 25 miles (40 km) from the nearest village.

In the center of France there is a magnificent group of volcanoes called the Puys. The Puys are a chain of cones crowned with craters, domes, and lava flows. The youngest of these are only a few thousand years old. In the foreground are the Puys of Vache and of Lassolas. These two craters were formed 8,200 years ago.

However, 3,500 years for a volcano are not even one night of human life! Volcanologists predict that an eruption will occur in the Massif Central within the next three thousand years. It will probably occur in the Puys, a chain of volcanoes west of Clermont-Ferrand. There, one hundred very recent volcanoes line great fissures. Most of them are cinder cones. Cinder cones are known for large lava flows. But around twenty of them are explosion craters, and four of them have domes of pasty lava.

The two highest French volcanoes are the Cantal and Mount Dore. The Cantal stands at 6,086 feet (1,855 m). It is a huge cone with gentle slopes. Today, it is very worn and scattered by rivers. Mount Dore is 6,184 feet (1,885 m) tall. It has a large crater at its center, caused by a collapse.

France, however, has three active volcanoes. They are located on its far away islands. The most famous, Mount Pelée in Martinique, killed 28,000 people in 1902. Not far away, in Guadeloupe, the Soufrière had huge explosions in 1976. Finally, on Réunion Island, Piton de la Fournaise has an eruption almost every year. These three volcanoes are permanently watched by volcanologists who work in observatories.

Do new volcanoes appear sometimes?

The birth of a volcano is a rare event. It is one which very few people witness. In 1538, Mount Nuovo arose in the middle of a village near Naples, Italy. You can imagine the fright of the people who saw this.

In 1943 in Mexico, a peasant working in his cornfield saw the earth suddenly open. Terrified, he ran away immediately. The next day, he was shocked to find a volcanic cone, 33 feet (10 m) high, furiously exploding in his field. He called it Paricutin, after the nearby village. The volcano, which spewed liquid lava, did not stop growing. One year later, it had reached a height of 1,102 feet (336 m). Paricutin was active for nine years. In that time, it buried its surroundings under thick layers of ash. It also engulfed two villages in its lava flows.

In 1944, the village of Fukaba, Japan, suffered many earthquakes. Little by little, the ground began to raise in a meadow and in the village. The roads and the houses cracked. Soon the village was abandoned. By the middle of the year, the little town sat high atop a great peak. Still the mound continued to grow. The new hill was named Showa Shinzan. It was soon 492 feet (150 m) high.

The ruins of the church of San Juan in Mexico mark the location of a town destroyed by Paricutin's lava flows. The volcano formed in the middle of a cornfield in 1943 (see top picture).

This view of Showa Shinzan (right) shows the volcano's huge bulge, covered with forests. The dome of smoking lava pierced it in 1944.

Soon a dome of pasty lava arose, growing like a giant mushroom out of the ground. The temperature in the area reached 1,652°F (900°C). In the end, Showa Shinzan dominated the plain at a height of 984 feet (300 m).

In 1963, while at sea south of Iceland, a ship's cook spotted smoke in the distance. At first he thought it was perhaps a ship on fire, but the ship had received no distress signal. Very soon, the crew smelled a strange odor. It was sulphur. Before them, a volcano was coming to the surface. This volcano, later named Surtsey, continued its violent eruptions for four years.

Which are the largest volcanoes on the earth?

The highest volcanoes in the world are found in the Andes Mountains in South America. The Republic of Ecuador also has some very high volcanoes, including Cotopaxi. This volcano is 19,347 feet (5,897 m) high. Its peak is covered with glaciers. They make it easy to spot the volcano from very far away. When it erupts, part of the ice melts, causing terrible mud flows.

The largest of all active volcanoes in the world is Mauna Loa. It is found in the Hawaiian Islands of the Pacific Ocean. Specifically, Mauna Loa sits in Hawaii Volcanoes National Park on the "big island" of Hawaii. This volcano is 13,677 feet (4,169 m) high. It has a diameter, at sea level, of 62 miles (100 km). But, in fact, it rests on the bottom of the ocean where it has a diameter of 155 miles (250 km). Measuring from the ocean floor, Mauna Loa is actually 29,856 feet (9,100 m) high. It is one of the highest points in the state. Mauna Loa has been active for almost one million years. It is one of Hawaii's two active volcanoes. It has had forty eruptions over 150 years.

The largest continental volcano is Kilimanjaro at 19,350 feet (5,898 m) high in Africa. It is dormant, or inactive, at present. Its volume is ten times less than Mauna Loa's, but ten times larger than Mount Etna's, which is Sicily's very active volcano.

The highest continental volcanoes are found in Chile. The volcano called Nevado Ojos de Salado is 22,588 feet (6,885 m) high. It is also dormant. Its neighbor, Llullaillaco, is 22,057 feet (6,723 m) high. It is still active.

Volcano heights are measured from sea level to their peaks. In this, Chile's volcanoes beat all others. But this is only because they were formed on mountains. The mountains were already 16,404 feet (5,000 m) high. The volcanoes' actual heights are not more than 6,562 feet (2,000 m).

Which are the largest craters on the planet?

The largest crater in the world, Garita, is found in the United States. It is 28 miles (45 km) in diameter. Next on the list is the Buldir in Alaska, with 19 miles (30 km). Craters Taupo in New Zealand, and Aso in Japan are both 12 miles (20 km) wide.

The crater of Santorini, in Greece, formed after a huge eruption around 1,500 B.C. It measures 11 miles by 7 miles (17 km by 11 km). It was flooded by the sea. The crater of Piton de la Fournaise on Réunion Island is 7 miles (11 km) long and 4 miles (6 km) wide. As for the crater of Vesuvius, it is only 1,969 feet (600 m) in diameter.

When craters are more than a mile in diameter, volcanologists call them calderas. This means cauldrons in Portuguese and Spanish.

Most of the craters are formed by the lava which gushes out of the volcano. It falls to earth around the mouth of the volcano, building a ring of ash and rocks. But some craters are formed by the explosion.

Calderas are rarely caused by explosions. They are often due to a collapse of a section of the volcano. When there are great eruptions, the magma reservoirs empty out very quickly. They suddenly become huge caves. Their ceilings are no longer supported by the magma. They cave in, creating the huge calderas at the surface.

Mauna Loa, in Hawaii, is the largest active volcano in the world. It is also the highest, if measured from the bottom of the Pacific Ocean up to its summit. The distance is 29,856 feet (9,100 m). Its caldera is also impressive. It has a length of 3 miles (4.8 km), a width of 1½ miles (2.4 km), and a depth of 656 feet (200 m). But these measurements are not on the list of records. The volcano's bottom is full of cones, flows, and eruptive fissures. These are proof of Mauna Loa's recent activities.

Are some volcanoes connected to each other?

Choungou Chahalé is the steep-sided crater of the Kartala Volcano. Kartala is found at Grande Comore in the Indian Ocean. On the bottom is a little cone of scoriae, or cindery lava. The terrace which overhangs it in the background marks the level of the crater's previous floor. The crater sinks a little with each collapse.

Years ago, Jules Verne wrote a book titled *Journey to the Center of the Earth.* In it, he describes the adventures of Professor Lindenbrock. In the book, the professor goes down the chimney of Sneffels Volcano in Iceland. After many adventures, he comes out again through the crater of Stromboli in Italy. Such a trip is completely imaginary. First, deep down, the volcanic chimneys are not hollow. Secondly, the heat of a volcano is unbearable. Finally, these two volcanoes are not connected to each other.

However, on May 8, 1902, the volcano of Mount Pelée at Martinique erupted, killing 28,000 people. Only 99 miles (160 km) away, the Soufrière of Saint Vincent had erupted the day before. That disaster killed two thousand people.

On May 29, 1937, at Rabaul, New Guinea, the volcano Vulcan erupted. A day later, Tavurvur, 4 miles (6 km) away, became very active. In this region in 1974, five volcanoes —all very close to one another— awoke in less than eight months.

There are also strange facts about volcanoes of the Indian Ocean. On September 7, 1972, Piton de la Fournaise on Réunion Island erupted. This volcano is active every year or every other year. Less than twenty-four hours later, Kartala of the Comores Islands did the same. This volcano is 1,054 miles (1,700 km) away. It usually erupts only twice every ten years. Then on April 5, 1977, a great eruption started along Kartala's sides . It destroyed the village of Singani. Five and a half hours later, the Piton de la Fournaise also erupted.

This does not mean that there is a direct connection between volcanoes. Instead, a rise in lava deposits probably sets off great volcanic areas.

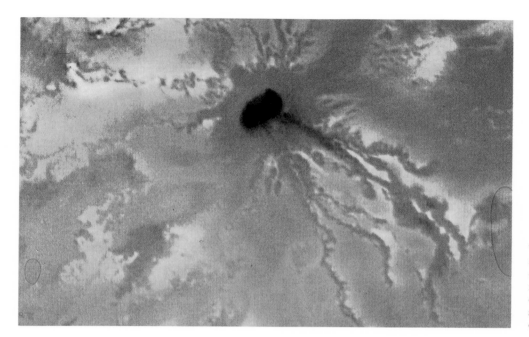

The surface of Io, one of Jupiter's satellites, has many volcanic eruptions. These eruptions are much greater than those on the earth. They release long flows of sulphur and spout gigantic plumes of gas.

Are there volcanoes on other planets?

You are probably familiar with meteors. These are the small, rocky particles that float in the solar system. Sometimes meteors fall to earth. Meteors that make it to earth are called meteorites. Some of them are made of cooled lava. Scientists think that these meteorites probably came from volcanoes on other planets.

American and Russian space missions have gained much information about volcanoes on other planets. Their findings show volcanic activity in the beginnings of several planets in the solar system. The moon, for example, is made of basalt. Basalt is the most common kind of earth lava. The bottoms of many of the moon's craters are full of it. The moon's volcanoes were active three or four billion years ago. But the moon's craters do not come from eruptions. They were formed when large meteors hit the moon.

The planet Mars is scattered with huge volcanoes. The largest of these volcanoes is Mount Olympus. This volcano is 434 miles (700 km) in diameter and 16 miles (25 km) high. Many volcanologists dream of climbing it one day. On Mars, some lava flows have stretched over 496 miles (800 km) long.

Mercury's surface resembles the moon's. It is marked by millions of craters. These were also caused by falling meteorites. Mysterious Venus is always hidden behind clouds. Scientists think it is an active planet. It has probably had recent volcanic eruptions.

Finally, Jupiter and Saturn are made mainly of gaseous elements. In 1979, American space probes took pictures of Jupiter's satellites. Satellites are planets or other bodies which orbit another, larger body. The pictures showed that one of the satellites, Io, has eight volcanoes. All eight are fully active. Volcanic eruptions had never before been photographed anywhere but on the earth.

This flow is from the Piton de la Fournaise. The glowing lava is still very hot and fluid. The older, cooled lava has become black stone.

Basalt sometimes comes to the surface from several miles deep. It often carries pieces of volcanic rock with it. These rocks come from the earth's mantle. This is true of these greenish rocks (below). These rocks, called peridotites, are rich in crystals. There are many of them in the flow pictured here.

What is lava?

When magma reaches the earth's surface, it is called lava. Lava is then molten rock. It is very hot, more or less soft, and comes from the earth's depths. When it cools, it hardens. It is then called volcanic rock. Depending on what it is made of, it is called basalt, andesite, rhyolite . . . .

Lava contains glass similar to window glass. This glass is mixed with iron, aluminum, calcium, magnesium, salts, and other elements. When cooled, these substances form crystals. This process is much like freezing water into ice.

If the lava has less than fifty percent glass in it, it is very fluid and very hot. This is called basalt. It is a black heavy rock because it has much iron in it. If it contains about sixty percent glass, it does not flow very well. It is then called andesite and is a gray rock. Finally, if it has more than sixty-five percent glass in it, it becomes very thick. This rock is called rhyolite and is a white or pink color.

Pumice and obsidian

During the seventh century A.D., there was an eruption on the island of Lipari in Italy. The volcano first spit out a light, foamy lava. This lava, called pumice, slid down the volcano's slopes. Later, a heavier, glassier liquid, called obsidian, followed. This type of eruption can be compared to opening a bottle of soda. Foam flows out first, followed by the liquid. The foamy pumice is usually white and full of gas bubbles. The gas makes it light enough to float on water. Obsidian is true volcanic glass. It is usually black. Prehistoric people once used obsidian for making tools.

What kinds of stones are found on volcanoes?

Cooled lava, or volcanic rock, is often black, gray, or white. If you look closely at the rocks, you will see beautiful crystals in them. There may be black bars of pyroxene, green beads of olivine, and white sheets of feldspar. During certain explosions, it rains pyroxene crystals. They sprinkle the volcano's summit. Large blocks of lava are sometimes called volcanic bombs. These bombs sometimes contain large bottle-green balls. These are made of hundreds of olivine beads stuck together. In Hawaii, there are whole beaches made of olivine crystals. The crystals were once used as jewelry.

The lava of certain South African volcanoes contains millions of diamond crystals. They were formed at 155 miles (250 km) down. There the temperature is 3,632°F (2,000°C) and the pressure is great. Rising magma pushed the diamond crystals to the surface.

The multicolored crystals are more common. These are found around the gas vents of many craters. These crystals include: the yellow sulphur, the fibers of white gypsum, and the piles of red iron salt. Sometimes, before reaching the surface, the gases pass through the volcanic rocks. They fill the gaps with beautiful white crystals. These are shaped like needles, cubes, or sheets.

Geysers are water springs. Geysers are like volcanoes in that both erupt. But geysers do not shoot out lava like volcanoes. Instead, they spew hot water. You are likely to find geyserite near geysers. Geyserite is a kind of milky glass. It is often very beautifully shaped. Other springs deposit limestone. Limestone covers everything with a hard, white crust. These springs are called "petrifactive springs."

Crystals are not always easy to find. If you are not lucky enough to find them, gather lava bombs and volcanic rocks instead. These are also interesting. Both can tell you much about the history of the volcano.

Katia Krafft, volcanologist, wears a mask while working near the volcano. The mask filters gas from the air. She also uses a small thermocouple. The thermocouple is a thermometer for measuring volcanic gas temperatures. Here she measures the gases escaping from Usu Volcano in Japan. These gases are very rich in sulphur. The sulphur settles, covering the vent area with beautiful needle-shaped stones.

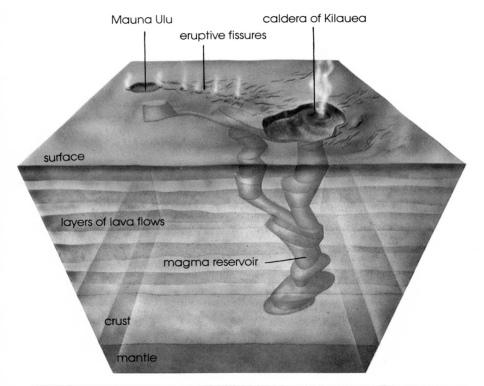

Mauna Ulu · eruptive fissures · caldera of Kilauea

surface

layers of lava flows

magma reservoir

crust

mantle

The magma reservoir beneath Kilauea Volcano in Hawaii (top) is located at a shallow depth. It was studied by volcanologists. As in most volcanoes, the form is very complex. The volcano's underground "plumbing" is made up of twisting and turning magma-filled channels.

(Bottom) Stromboli in Italy has been almost permanently active for more than two thousand years. Near its summit, several small craters explode regularly. This delights the many tourists who climb it.

From what depth does the lava come?

Lava often comes from a depth of 19 to 50 miles (30 to 80 km). There a layer of magma lies hidden beneath the earth's crust. But this depth varies, depending on the type of volcano.

Some volcanoes have small reservoirs near the earth's surface. Magma gathers there. Vesuvius in Italy, for example, has a reservoir 3 miles (5 km) down. Mount Etna in Sicily has one at 12 miles (20 km). Krafla in Iceland has a reservoir just 2 miles (3 km) down. On the other hand, some volcanoes have very deep chambers. Stromboli in Italy has magma that comes from 155 miles (250 km) deep.

In Hawaii, Kilauea's magma comes from a depth of 31 miles (50 km). It rises through its chimney to a reservoir 2½ miles (4 km) from the surface. It gathers there until the volcano erupts. Each day, more magma rises and flows into the chamber.

Today, volcanologists know that many reservoirs are close to the surface. Under the famous geysers of Yellowstone National Park in the United States, the magma is only 4 miles (6 km) from the surface. This location may someday be very useful. With drills, scientists will tap into the magma chambers. They will build powerful stations to capture and use the earth's great heat.

These magma reservoirs have different, often complicated shapes. Some are very long. Others are a series of tubes that turn in every direction. Still other reservoirs are made up of tiny cavities and fissures in the rocks. Magma soaks into these holes like water into a sponge.

How hot is lava?

Lava flows down the volcano's slopes in long, glowing rivers. These flows can reach temperatures of 2,192°F (1,200°C). Water boils at 212°F (100°C). Thus flowing lava can reach temperatures over ten times hotter than boiling water. To understand how hot this is, imagine throwing a pair of shoes into the lava. They would burn, melt, and disappear in less than a minute.

At night, you can sometimes guess at the lava's temperature just by its color. The red lava ranges from 1,472° to 1,832°F (800° to 1,000°C). Orange is usually between 1,832° and 2,102°F (1,000° to 1,150°C). Yellow lava is the hottest at 2,102° to 2,192°F (1,150° to 1,200°C).

To find the exact temperature of a flow, the volcanologist uses a special thermometer. It is called a thermocouple. Sometimes it is too dangerous to go near the lava. Then the lava's temperature is measured from far away with electronic binoculars.

Maurice Krafft, volcanologist, sometimes wears a fire-resistant suit in his studies. This suit protects him from the lava's heat. Here he uses a thermocouple to measure the lava's temperature. This particular lava flow is from an eruption on Piton de la Fournaise on Réunion Island. Its hardened crust had to be broken to reach the molten rock. The temperature of the lava was 2,093°F (1,145°C).

In a deep channel, this flow from Mount Etna is protected from the cool air. This keeps the lava very hot. It is about 2,102°F (1,150°C) where it is yellow. The dark red lava is less hot at 1,800°F (1,000° C). The heat keeps the lava very fluid. It continues to flow at 6 miles (10 km) an hour.

Lava escaped from the crater of Nyiragongo in Zaïre on January 10, 1977. The lava was so hot that it flowed faster than 25 miles (40 km) an hour. It even surprised a herd of elephants, engulfing them. In time, the elephants' bodies disappeared. This left only their bones and a hole. As you can see, the hole is a perfect mold, or casting, of each elephant. You can pick out the body, the legs, the tail, and even the trunk of the animal.

How fast does lava flow?

A lava flow's speed depends on many things. What it is made of is one factor. The more glass it contains, the thicker it is. The lava's temperature is also important. The hotter a flow is, the faster it moves. Finally, there is the volcano's slope to consider. Steeper slopes will move the lava quicker.

The most common type of lava flow is made of basalt. Basalt can flow at about the same speed that a person can run. However, at Mauna Loa and Kilauea in Hawaii, the lava flows much faster. There it can flow as fast as 50 miles (80 km) an hour.

In 1938, the lava from Nyamuragira in Zaïre caught up with antelopes. In the same region in 1977, a lava lake suddenly emptied from the crater of Nyiragongo. The lava ran out open fissures and down the volcano's sides. It reached a speed of 37 miles (60 km) an hour. Many villagers who tried to run were caught, burned, and buried by the molten lava. A herd of elephants had the same fate. Today, their shapes are cast in the lava. The rock preserves their forms like modeling clay captures a thumb print.

But these are special cases. Usually the flows slow down just several hundred feet from the volcano's mouth. This is true even when the lava gushes from the mouth very quickly. Normally, lava moves no faster than the speed of a person walking slowly. Some flows are even slower than that. These may move only a few feet per hour. So generally, people can escape a lava flow.

How far does lava flow from a volcano?

Very thick lava never flows very far. It tends to gather at the chimney exit, forming a dome. The more fluid flows are generally basalt. They go down the volcano's valleys like rivers. Some of them spread out as far as the plains. There they cover large areas before cooling down and hardening.

The largest known flow was from the huge fissure of Laki Volcano in Iceland. The lava ran 37 miles (60 km) from the volcano. Then, spreading out, it covered 193 square miles (500 sq. km). During the first few days of the eruption, the flow moved very fast. Its speed was twice as fast as some great rivers flow at their mouths.

About 14 million years ago, lava flows covered the western United States. They ran 186 miles (300 km) in a few days. In the end, the lava buried several thousand square miles of land.

Huge surfaces of India, the United States, and South America are covered with thousands of feet of lava flows. In India, lava flows cover 96,525 sq. miles (250,000 sq. km) of the Deccan plateau. In South America, lava covers 77,220 sq. miles (200,000 sq. km) of Brazil and Patagonia. In the United States, the Columbia River plain has 46,332 sq. miles (120,000 sq. km) of lava flows. This amount alone would be enough to cover Belgium, France, and Switzerland with a layer of lava a half-mile thick.

The flows of Piton de la Fournaise are small compared to those of Mauna Loa in Hawaii. Still, this volcano's flows are able to totally cover large land masses. Even old volcanic cones are buried in a few days. Thus a volcano can totally change an area's physical features within a few weeks.

How long does it take for lava to cool?

A thin, hard layer forms over lava in the first hour of its cooling. This is very much like a lake as it begins to freeze. Volcanologists sometimes walk on this hardened carapace, or covering, of rock. In places, it may be less than an inch thick. Just beneath this layer, the lava is still as hot as 1,832°F (1,000°C). It is still molten and continues to move.

In spots the crust is cracked and open. You can look through the glowing fissures and see lava running into tunnels. The ground is very hot. The soles of your shoes melt and stick like chewing gum. If you spit on the ground, the saliva is immediately turned into steam!

When the first crust forms, it encloses the rest of the lava. Now the inner lava will begin to cool. This process is a very slow one.

A picnic on a lava flow

In 1920, a volcanologist had an interesting adventure on Kilauea Volcano. He had chosen a comfortable spot in the middle of a still lukewarm lava rock to have lunch. While eating, he looked around. The countryside seemed to be moving. He suddenly realized that he was sitting on a moving lava flow. Not at all worried, he quietly finished his meal.

Lava will lose its heat quickly if it is only 3 to 7 feet (1 to 2 m) thick. Still, it will need about a month to cool to the center. But it may take ten months to cool lava that is 50 feet (15 m) thick. Some lava is even thicker—perhaps even 328 feet (100 m). It may take several centuries for this lava to cool.

A 1973 eruption at Heimaey in Iceland destroyed part of the city. Today, the people tap the lava flows for their heat. Ten years later there is still a great amount of heat in them. The people use this energy to heat their homes.

The inside of the lava flow often contracts when cooling down. The lava then becomes fissured like dry soil. It divides into long basalt columns. Eventually water may clean out these cooled flows. Then the columns become visible. An example of this can be found at Gomera, in the Canary Islands.

These beautiful pillars of lava are called basalt columns. They come from the inside of old flows. These are found at Gomera in the Canary Islands. Little by little, the waves of the sea have eroded the surface of the flow, revealing the interior.

Are all lava flows the same?

Not all lava flows are the same. What kind of flow comes from an eruption depends on several things. Among them are: what a flow is made of, how much gas is in it, and the temperature of the flow. Volcanologists separate flows into three main types: smooth flows, coarse flows, and block flows.

The smooth flows are continuous, generally not very thick streams of lava. Sometimes they are slab-like. Often, they are folded in the shape of ropes or glassy, shining rolls. Smooth flows are called *pahoehoe* (pronounced *pah HOH ee HOH ee*), which means "satiny" in the Hawaiian language.

The coarse flows are broken, thick masses of lava. They form rough, cindery piles of lava called scoriae. These flows are called *aa* (AH ah). This word is also from the Hawaiian language. The aa flows cool to rough, jagged rocks. They move like large rock piles pushed by bulldozers.

The block flows are very thick. They are made up of compact, jagged rocks. Often these move like rock falls. Block flows are found in particular on volcanoes releasing thick lava. The other two types of flows are more fluid.

In addition to these three types of lava flows there are also the underwater flows. These, you may remember, take the form of pillows piled one on top of the other.

A flow of basaltic lava that is very hot and has a smooth surface is called a pahoehoe flow. When a flow like this folds, it takes the shape of ropes and sausages. These flows, at Piton de la Fournaise on Réunion Island (upper left) and at Mauna Ulu, Hawaii (upper right), are examples of a pahoehoe flow.

A sticky, coarse flow can be rough, crumbled, and full of gas bubbles. This type of flow is called an aa flow. It moves like a pile of rocks pushed by a bulldozer. This is true of this orchard on Etna buried in 1983 (lower left).

The very thick flows are known as block flows. Block flows are often made of andesite rock. This type of flow piles up in huge, jagged blocks, as at Sakurajima, Japan, in 1914 (lower right).

What does a volcano eject when it erupts?

During an eruption, a volcano ejects, or releases, gases. These gases cause the explosions. Then the volcano throws, or projects, lava. Lava can be soft or hard, and of all different sizes. Volcanologists separate volcanic materials by their size. From the smallest to the largest they include dust, ashes, lapilli, and blocks.

Volcanic dust is made up of lava particles as fine as flour. The dust from an eruption can be carried very far. Volcanic ash, or cinder, is a slightly larger type of lava. It is made of lava fragments and resembles sand. At times, the ash mixes with water and forms a boiling mudflow.

Both lapilli and blocks are larger forms of lava. The word *lapilli* is an Italian word meaning "little stones." Lapilli can reach the size of tennis balls. Volcanic blocks generally range from baseball to basketball size, but actually have no limit. These large fragments are sometimes called volcanic bombs.

When the lapilli and the blocks are full of gas bubbles, they form scoriae. Sometimes there are many bubbles. The scoriae becomes very light and sponge-like. It is then called pumice. At this stage, the lava is like foam and floats on the water.

Bombs are blocks with specific shapes. Some of them are shaped like spindles, with thick middles and long, thin ends. Others are called cow dung bombs. These

In 1983, the ash plumes of Galunggung in Indonesia rose several miles high. When the volcanic dust fell back to earth, it blocked the sunlight. The country was plunged into darkness at high noon (upper left photograph).

Volcanic bombs take many shapes. Mount Asama in Japan threw breadcrust shaped bombs (upper right photograph). Red Top in Alaska ejected spindle-shaped bombs (lower right photograph). Spindle-shaped bombs form when the lava is still soft. The lava pieces stretch at both ends as they hurtle through the air.

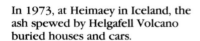

In 1973, at Heimaey in Iceland, the ash spewed by Helgafell Volcano buried houses and cars.

spread smoothly over the ground when they fall. Still others are cauliflower shaped. The surfaces of these bombs puff up when they touch water. This makes them look like the vegetable. Finally, some volcanic bombs look like breadcrusts. The coverings of these bombs crack as the lava cools.

The bombs can be huge. Still, they often fall far from the volcano's mouth. Asama in Japan threw a breadcrust type bomb half a mile (1 km). The bomb was 39 feet (12 m) around and weighed 1,600 tons.

Dust, ashes, lapilli and blocks usually fall back to earth right around the active volcano's mouth. There they pile up, rapidly crowning the volcanic cones with craters. In 1975, the cone of Tolbachik, in Russia, rose 1,969 feet (600 m) in four months. But very violent explosions can shoot ashes and dust very far from the volcano.

Do the volcanic projections go up very high?

Blocks and lapilli do not shoot much higher than a few thousand feet. They go up a mile or two at the most. This is true even during gigantic explosions. But ash, and especially volcanic dust, can go up much higher. They are much lighter.

During Krakatoa's famous eruption in 1883, the plume of volcanic dust rose 25 miles (40 km) high! The volcanic projections were put "into orbit" in the high atmosphere. Pushed by strong winds, they went around the globe three times. Most of the earth's surface was sprinkled with Krakatoa's volcanic powder.

The all-time record was set in 186 A.D. by the volcano Taupo in New Zealand. It has been estimated that the dust from that eruption rose 31 miles (50 km) high.

In 1980, Mount St. Helens in the United States (Washington state) threw a dozen plumes of ash 12 miles (20 km) high. On July 22, 1980, for example, three explosions shot dust 11 miles (18 km) high. Two weeks later, the dust clouds sprinkled eastern France and Switzerland like a thin layer of snow. Pushed by westerly winds, the ash from Mount St. Helens crossed the Atlantic Ocean in the high atmosphere. It traveled close to 9,300 miles (15,000 km) in twelve days.

Finally, in 1982, El Chichon in Mexico erupted twice, spewing ash and sulphur gases 22 miles (35 km) high. The volcano had been dormant more than one hundred years.

This eruption formed a cloud 4,960 miles (8,000 km) long. The cloud circled the earth for more than a year. It moved from east to west at 50 miles (80 km) an hour.

On July 22, 1980, a plume of blocks, ashes and gases rose from Mount St. Helens. It shot 11 miles (18 km) high in a few minutes. Columns of volcanic matter are often called "plinian plumes." They were named in honor of Pliny the Younger, who observed and described the eruption of Vesuvius in 79 A.D.

What is a glowing cloud?

Glowing clouds poured out of the crater of El Chichon in April, 1982. The clouds then went down the volcano's sides and filled valleys with huge grayish masses. These masses were 98 feet (30 m) thick. They were still warm a year later.

On May 8, 1982, Mount Pelée in Martinique erupted. An enormous avalanche of blocks, gases, and glowing ash hurtled down the volcano's slopes. The mass moved at a speed of 93 miles (150 km) an hour. It razed the town of Saint Pierre within two minutes and killed 28,000 people. This kind of avalanche has been named "glowing cloud." It is the most deadly of volcanic eruptions. These glowing clouds have killed more than sixty thousand people in two thousand years.

At Mayon in the Philippine Islands, volcanologists observed glowing clouds rolling at a speed of 136 miles (220 km) an hour. These clouds destroyed everything in their path. Gliding on a layer of air, they moved over the ground as easily as an avalanche of snow.

The 1980 eruption of Mount St. Helens included an enormous blast from the volcano's side. This is called a horizontal blast. This eruption also included glowing clouds. Together, the explosions and the glowing clouds destroyed pine forests up to 19 miles (30 km) away. The glowing clouds moved at speeds of 186 miles (300 km) an hour and buried sixty-five people.

Glowing clouds form when an ash plume becomes too heavy to rise. Instead, it collapses into an avalanche.

In great explosions, glowing clouds cover huge areas in a few hours. They flow like milk boiling over a pan. Along the way, they bury everything under a thick layer of ash and pumice.

The only recent eruption of this importance was in 1912. That year, Katmai Volcano in Alaska released 2 cu. miles (10 cu. km) of volcanic ash. In twenty hours, the ash filled a valley 12 miles (20 km) long and 2 miles (4 km) wide to a thickness of 98 feet (30 m). When explorers reached the site four years later, it was still smoking everywhere. They called it "the Valley of Ten Thousand Smokes." Thirty thousand years ago, a similar eruption took place in Naples, Italy. That eruption was many times greater, however.

Do volcanoes release a lot of gas?

Volcanoes are huge natural factories. They constantly release gases that become trapped in their magma. These gases include: carbon dioxide, hydrogen, sulphur dioxide, and other mixtures with unpleasant odors.

During eruptions, volcanoes often release huge amounts of gas. In 1783, Laki Volcano in Iceland was active for eight months. In that time, it let off a huge amount of steam vapor. But it also released, or emitted, 100 million tons of sulphuric gas and 20 million tons of carbon dioxide gas.

During their dormant periods, volcanoes release less gases. These leave through fissures opened here and there in the craters. Certain holes that release only gases and vapors are called *fumaroles*.

Volcanologists can estimate the amount of gases a volcano releases in a year. They have even figured the total amount of gas given off from all volcanoes on earth in a year. They estimate this amount to be at least ten billion billion tons. Now, consider that volcanoes have existed for 4.5 billion years. In that time, they have spewed all the water (in the form of steam) contained in the seas, lakes and rivers of the earth. The carbon dioxide, the hydrogen, and the nitrogen gases they have released fill the atmosphere.

The carbon dioxide is especially important. Plants change this gas into oxygen. Without this oxygen, people could not live. So without volcanoes, there would be no water or atmosphere on this planet. Without these things, there would be no life.

In 1973, Eldfell Volcano in southern Iceland erupted. An enormous plume of steam and gases rose from the new volcano. This plume, which could be seen from boats at sea, announced the volcano to the world.

Green, blue, and red sun

During very large volcanic explosions, huge amounts of dust particles shoot high into the atmosphere. These mix with the sun's rays, creating beautiful green, blue, and blood red sunrises and sunsets. For example, ash thrown from Krakatoa in 1883 drifted over the United States. The sun and the dust mixed to set the sky aglow. The glow was so great that firemen in New Haven, Connecticut actually went looking for a fire.

Do volcanoes pollute?

Active craters spew large amounts of gas. But factories release six times more carbon dioxide gas and ten times more gases rich in sulphur than all the volcanoes on earth. An average eruption produces less poisonous gas than a coal-burning electrical plant.

However, the gas and dust from active volcanoes can be dangerous to people. For example, on February 20, 1979, a small crater opened on a plateau in Indonesia. It suddenly erupted with a deafening blast, spewing gases and blocks. The people of a village nearby panicked and fled. But they did not escape. A blanket of poisonous gas rose from

Since its awakening in 1955, Sakurajima Volcano in Japan has erupted many times. Its plumes of ash and gas are sometimes blown back onto the island by the wind. Over the years, these plumes have destroyed many fields. At times, they have filled the surrounding areas with unbreathable air. One day, there may be a great eruption. The island's ten thousand people may then need to flee quickly. They have made plans for this. They have also built shelters and special harbors for the rescuers.

the crater. It crossed the road just as the people passed. The gas killed all of them.

The largest disaster caused by volcanic gas took place in Iceland. This happened during the eruption of Laki in 1783. The volcano's sulphur gas burned and destroyed more than a third of the country. Fluorine gas, which is poisonous, infected the drinking water and the grass. It killed 11,000 cattle, 200,000 sheep, and 28,000 horses. A food shortage followed and ten thousand people died. At the time, that was one-fourth of the population.

Laki also released a huge amount of gas and dust. It created a thick fog that settled over all of Europe. The fog blocked the sun's rays for months. That winter was one of the coldest of the century.

In 1815, the volcano Tambora in Indonesia erupted. It disturbed the earth's climate and caused many problems. The explosion threw millions of tons of gas and dust into the high atmosphere. This created a cloud that blocked the sun's rays for a long time. Because of this, 1816 has often been called "the year without summer." In the eastern United States it snowed in June, froze in August, and rained every day from May to October. The harvest was lost and a terrible food shortage followed.

What is a geyser?

When a volcano is old, the magma no longer surges to the surface. It no longer has the force. In its chamber, it heats the rocks and water moving around it. Sometimes, through fissures, this boiling water rises to the surface. It shoots out in large bursts. This is called a geyser.

An example of this can be found in Yellowstone National Park in the northwestern United States. There a reservoir of magma is found 4 miles (6 km) below the surface. This magma heats two hundred geysers in the area. This number represents half of all the geysers in the world.

For many years, the Stori Geysir of Iceland shot a beautiful spray of water 230 feet (70 m) high. It gave geysers their name. *Geysir* comes from the Icelandic verb *gjosa* which means "gush forth." Today, the Stori Geysir is dormant.

The highest geyser of all time was the Waimangu, in New Zealand. It was active from 1900 to 1904. Every thirty hours, it threw steam, muddy water, and rock fragments 1,476 feet (450 m) into the air. Today, the record seems to be at Steamboat Geyser in Yellowstone. This geyser surges 393 feet (120 m) into the air. Nearby is the famous geyser, "Old Faithful." Since 1878, without stopping, it has spouted its water 197 feet (60 m) high for two to five minutes. After thirty to one hundred minutes, it begins again.

How a geyser works is complex and still not very well understood. The geyser's water is trapped in an underground chamber. This chamber is found hundreds of feet below the surface. There the water is heated. Boiling, it moves into the channels and tubes which carry it to the surface. There, the pressure is reduced. The water is changed into steam. As this happens, its mass suddenly increases many times. With that, the geyser explodes.

Soap and geysers

In 1880, a Chinese laundryman decided to use the hot water from a spring at Yellowstone to wash his clothes. In a pool, he began to soap his clothes. Suddenly the pool spouted all of its water into a great geyser! It is now known that soap bubbles can cause a geyser. Soap makes many bubbles. When these bubbles gather together, they rise and force all the water into the channels. Since this experience, soap has often been used to awaken some geysers on command.

The Strokkur Geyser is at present the highest geyser in Iceland. It was purposely opened to replace the great Stori Geysir. That geyser is no longer active.

What is a solfatara?

Solfatara is Italian for "sulphur mine." It was originally the name of an old volcano near Vesuvius. This crater now shoots fountains of steam from fumaroles. It is full of pools of boiling mud. These pools gurgle with sulphur-rich gas.

The fumaroles change the rocks into different colored clay and crystal deposits. This gives a volcano multicolored walls. Today, the word solfatara refers to volcanic areas that are rich in sulphur. Like the geysers, solfataras usually form in old volcanoes.

The sulphur deposits are also called sulphur pits. The pits were mined for a long time. About 1860, workers dug hundreds of tons of sulphur from Volcano Island near Sicily every year. Earlier, Spanish conquistadors looked for sulphur at the bottom of Popocatepetl crater, in Mexico. The conquistadors used the sulphur for cannon powder.

Today, only some solfataras are mined for their sulphur. Most of these are found on volcanoes in Chile, Japan, and Indonesia. The crater lake of Kawah Idjen Volcano in Indonesia is one of these. The Indonesians, under difficult working conditions, gather four tons of sulphur each day.

On the edge of the Kawah Idjen crater in Indonesia, the fumaroles spit great amounts of sulphur. The Indonesian people gather four tons of it each day. The sulphur is used to whiten sugar and to make rubber.

The six main types of volcanic eruptions (right page). It is not correct to say that a volcano is Hawaiian, Peléan, Vulcanian . . . . Instead, an eruption is Hawaiian, Peléan, or Vulcanian. A volcano that usually has one kind of eruption can even change.

Are all volcanic eruptions alike?

There are many different kinds of volcanic eruptions. To understand how one eruption differs from another, a volcanologist might ask these questions. Is the lava fluid or thick? Is it rich or poor in gases? Did water mix with the magma? All these things set one eruption apart from another.

Volcanologists separate eruptions into six types. These are: Hawaiian eruptions, Strombolian eruptions, fissural eruptions, Vulcanian eruptions, Peléan eruptions, and collapsed eruptions.

Sometimes the lava is very fluid. It spreads out in large flows or boils in lava lakes. This is called a Hawaiian eruption. It is named for the gently sloped volcanoes of the Hawaiian Islands. This type of eruption is common there. Sometimes, these eruptions begin as large fissures. They often run several miles long. The lava gushes out all along the fissure. Then it is called a fissural eruption.

At times, the lava is thicker. The eruptions will still have flows, but they will include explosions. This is

The different kinds of eruptions.

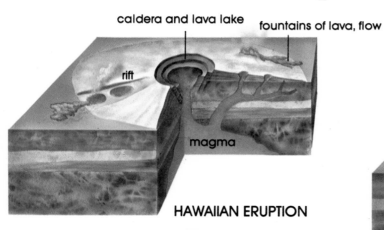

caldera and lava lake
fountains of lava, flow
rift
magma

HAWAIIAN ERUPTION

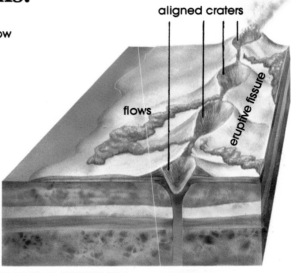

aligned craters
flows
eruptive fissure

FISSURAL ERUPTION
dike

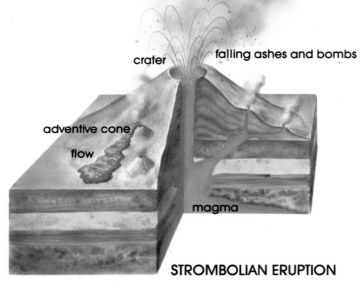

crater
falling ashes and bombs
adventive cone
flow
magma

STROMBOLIAN ERUPTION

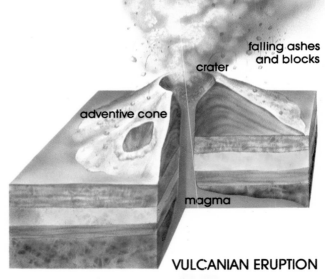

falling ashes and blocks
crater
adventive cone
magma

VULCANIAN ERUPTION

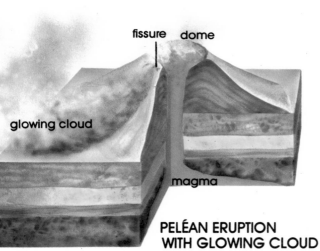

fissure   dome
glowing cloud
magma

**PELÉAN ERUPTION
WITH GLOWING CLOUD**

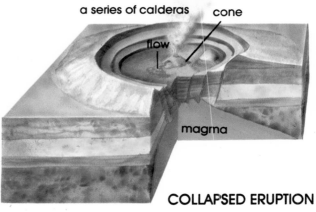

a series of calderas   cone
flow
magma

COLLAPSED ERUPTION

39

called a Strombolian eruption after the volcano Stromboli in Italy. When the lava is very thick, there are two possibilities. In the first case, there are powerful explosions of ash and rock. The dust rises in huge, dark umbrella clouds. These are Vulcanian eruptions. They are named after the Vulcano Volcano in northern Sicily. The flows are rare and often thick. In the second case, the molten rock forms a plug at the end of the volcano's chimney. The trapped gas pushes at the plug from below. This causes it to rise, slowly building a lava dome. Big clouds of gas, ash, and rocks, called glowing clouds, sometimes escape from the dome's fissures. The clouds slide down the slopes. This kind of eruption was seen at Mount Pelée in Martinique, in 1902. Since then, these eruptions have been called Peléan. When these eruptions are very violent, gigantic glowing clouds can cover huge amounts of land.

Finally, a volcano's summit sometimes collapses when the magma reservoir empties. This is called a collapsed eruption.

A volcano often has the same kind of eruption each time. However, it can change. For example, Vesuvius often has Strombolian eruptions. But it has also had Hawaiian, Vulcanian, and even Peléan activity.

Which volcano has the most eruptions?

The short but violent explosions of the Aso Volcano in Japan make it very dangerous. Still, thousands of visitors climb it every day. To be prepared for any disaster, anti-bomb shelters have been built on the crater's edges.

The most violent and the most active volcano on earth is French. It is the Piton de la Fournaise on Réunion Island in the Indian Ocean. This magnificent volcano has had eighty eruptions since the beginning of the century. During the same time, Kilauea Volcano in Hawaii has had fifty eruptions. Its neighbor, Mauna Loa, has had forty. After these come many famous volcanoes like Aso Volcano in Japan, Ngauruhoe Volcano in New Zealand, the Semeru and the Merapi volcanoes in Indonesia, and Mount Etna in Sicily. All of these have had close to twenty major eruptions in this century.

Of course, certain rare volcanoes have had almost continual activity for hundreds and even thousands of years. These include Stromboli Volcano in Italy, the Yasour in Vanuatu, and Erta Alé Volcano in Ethiopia.

How long does an eruption last?

An eruption can last from a few seconds to thousands of years. Sometimes a volcano oozes very thick lava. Such a volcano may explode suddenly. Its slow-moving lava builds great gas pressure beneath it. This type of eruption lasts only a few moments. With a blast, the volcano opens its crater. The pressure is released, and the eruption is over.

Other volcanoes have open chimneys. If a chimney is connected to the magma chamber, the lava can flow at any time. Such a crater will not stop exploding for years.

But these are two extremes. Volcanologists have found that most eruptions last three to four weeks. They are usually violent if the volcano has been dormant for a time.

The fountains of lava last only a few days during eruptions at Piton de la Fournaise. But the explosions and flows last several weeks.

High cliffs line the edge of Santorini's caldera in Greece. They were created during the gigantic eruption in 1,470 B.C. The cliffs are crowned with a white layer. This layer comes from the showers of pumice that also took place in that eruption.

Which were the biggest eruptions?

The two largest eruptions in history were at Santorini in Greece (1,470 B.C.), and at Taupo in New Zealand (186 A.D.). These two volcanoes crushed and ejected 6 cubic miles (25 cu. km) of volcanic material in a few hours. Santorini's eruption created a caldera that measures 7 miles (11 km) by 4 miles (7 km). It is 2,297 feet (700 m) deep. This explosion was followed by a great sea wave that hit the Mediterranean coast. This disaster may have destroyed the Minoan people living on the nearby island of Crete. Some people say this explains the sudden disappearance of the civilization.

In prehistoric times there were much larger eruptions than there are today. Thirty thousand years ago, the whole area of Naples, Italy, was buried in an eruption. In a few hours, ash and rock covered 2,703 sq. miles (7,000 sq. km) of land. Such disasters are still possible. Whole cities such as Rome, Mexico City, or even Portland could disappear in a few minutes.

But this is not even the greatest, or most amazing, of events. For example, 75,000 years ago, the Toba Volcano in Indonesia had a series of giant explosions. These explosions spewed miles of ash. They also created a caldera 62 miles (100 km) long and 19 miles (30 km) wide. At the height of the disaster, Toba's mouth shot out 130,787 cu. yards (100,000 cu. m) of lava per second. This is seven times the speed of the Amazon River, the largest river on earth.

But the record eruptions belong to volcanoes in the United States. Two million years ago, a volcano in Yellowstone National Park spewed 600 cu. miles (2,500 cu. km) of volcanic dust at once. The largest of the large was the eruption of Roza in Washington state. That flow's volume was 960 cu. miles (4,000 cu. km). It buried an area equal to the size of Switzerland.

Do volcanoes cause tidal waves?

In 1883, Krakatoa's eruption caused a tidal wave. The powerful wave uplifted a large gunboat, the *Berrouw,* and threw it far inland. The boat's metal boiler now lies in a river, behind a hill.

Plunging into a bathtub full of water causes waves which can overflow all around. These are like small tidal waves. You can imagine what happens when a volcano rises from the ocean or sinks with great force. The most famous case is that of Krakatoa. Krakatoa is a volcanic island in the Sunda Strait in Indonesia. In 1883, the volcano erupted with a terrible explosion. Explosions such as these sometimes create gigantic sea waves, called tidal waves. The tidal wave created by Krakatoa broke on the coasts of Java and Sumatra. It drowned 36,000 people.

The city of Teluk Betong, 43 miles (70 km) away, was also hit. The wave reached it at a height of 72 feet (22 m). It destroyed everything in its path. It even carried away a warship anchored in the harbor. The ship was later found 2 miles (3 km) inland. Even the island of Ceylon was hit by the wave. Ceylon is 2,170 miles (3,500 km) from Krakatoa. There, the wave was still strong enough to put boats on dry land. The wave was even recorded on the French coast of Brittany. By then it was 11,160 miles (18,000 km) from its origin.

Today, thousands of people again live along the coasts where their ancestors died in 1883. The tidal waves and other disasters do not frighten them away from the coasts. Instead, after each disaster, they simply rebuild—often in the same spots.

But volcanic eruptions are only one cause of tidal waves. Most of them are actually caused by earthquakes. The sudden movement of the coasts or ocean bottom often sets a wave in motion.

Can a strong earthquake cause an eruption?

It is rare that an earthquake directly causes an eruption. The Puyhue Volcano in Chile was dormant for fifty-five years. It erupted forty-eight hours after a huge Chilean earthquake on May 22, 1960. Hawaii's Kilauea Volcano released a lava flow forty-four minutes after a strong earthquake shook the region on November 29, 1975. In both cases, ground movements near the volcanoes caused the magma to rise. Pushed by gases, the magma caused eruptions. This is something like shaking a bottle of soda. This makes the bubbles rise within the liquid.

One volcanologist studied large earthquakes. The studies showed that earthquakes occurring even hundreds of miles beneath the surface can affect volcanoes. These earthquakes can cause magma to rise. But usually, volcanoes do not react to large earthquakes. The huge earthquake of Messine in 1908, for example, did not affect Mount Etna. The often violent quakes of southern Italy are another example. Despite their strength, they do not bother Vesuvius.

Many people confuse large earthquakes with volcanic eruptions. The two are very separate events. People may be confused because the two often happen in the same areas. Both eruptions and earthquakes occur where the earth's crust is fissured. But they are not alike and are not directly related.

Some earthquakes destroy entire towns. These are caused by long fissures opening with a jolt. Certainly active volcanoes shake. But this action is more like shivering. Every day, below the surface, volcanoes have small quakes. These are usually not destructive. Instead, they are caused by the movement of magma.

The earth vibrates

On May 22, 1960, a gigantic earthquake shook Chile. It was so strong that the whole earth shook, or vibrated. It vibrated for several weeks. This helped scientists understand the structure of the planet. The earth seems to be very rigid. Scientists now know that it is actually flexible and loses its shape easily. Land tides prove this. Like water bodies, the land can also have tides. The word tide simply refers to the change, or distortion, of one body that is caused by the gravitational pull of another. Every six hours, the earth changes. It rises or falls about 12 inches (30 cm). The moon's gravitational pull causes both these tides and those of the oceans.

On July 14, 1976, the earth shook in Bali, Indonesia. The houses collapsed. In a few minutes there was nothing but a pile of bricks and rubble at Séririt on the island's northern side. A few hours later, the Batur Volcano, nearby, awakened . . . .

Are eruptions deadly?

During the last five hundred years, volcanoes have killed 250,000 people. Eruptions claim an average of five victims a year. In the same time, larger earthquakes kill about ten thousand people.

Only six volcanoes' eruptions have caused ten thousand or more deaths. These include: Laki in Iceland (1783), Unzendake in Japan (1792), Mount Pelée in Martinique (1902), and Kelut (1586), Tambora (1815), and Krakatoa (1883), all of Indonesia.

The petrified victims of Pompeii

The archaeologist Giuseppe Fiorelli is credited with bringing order to the ruins of Pompeii. The Roman town, Pompeii, was destroyed in 79 A.D. An eruption from Mount Vesuvius covered it with a 20-foot (6 m) layer of volcanic ash. In digging, Fiorelli found imprints of the eruption's victims in the ash. After these people died, their bodies were buried beneath the ash. The bodies soon decomposed, but the hardened ash held their forms. Fiorelli made casts of the victims by pumping plaster into the molds. His work recreates the people the molds had contained. It captures the tragedy of Pompeii's last hour.

Mount Pelée in Martinique seems very quiet with its blanket of grass. However, it is a very explosive volcano. The lava dome at its summit dates from the eruption of 1929. This eruption was not deadly.

The most deadly eruption was Tambora's. It killed 92,000 people. Ten thousand of these people died beneath the blocks and ash thrown by the explosions. The rest died from the famine which followed. The famine resulted because plants no longer grew on the island. The volcano had destroyed all the fields.

The explosions of Krakatoa caused tidal waves. These drowned 36,000 Indonesians along the coast of the Sunda Strait.

The explosion of Mount Pelée in 1902 killed 28,000 people in two minutes. All of the people of St. Pierre died except for two men. Only a shoemaker and a prisoner in his cell survived.

The famous eruption of Mount Vesuvius took place in 79 A.D. This eruption buried the villages of Pompeii and Herculaneum. Two thousand people died. If this happened today, it would be ten times more deadly. The amount of people now living on Vesuvius' flanks is much greater.

Is an active volcano very noisy?

The noise from volcanic eruptions is often loud and frightening. It seems to come from the center of earth. The gases hiss. The flows crunch or hiss softly. The lava lakes rumble, and the explosions thunder. Of all this noise, only the explosions can be heard at a distance. They are sometimes strong enough to be heard thousands of miles away.

In 1835, for example, the people of Bogota, Columbia, heard the explosion of the volcano Cosegüina. Cosegüina, Nicaragua, is located 1,178 miles (1,900 km) away from them.

The explosions of Krakatoa were very strong. They broke window glass at a radius of 310 miles (500 km) around the volcano. This is the worst case recorded during the last hundred years.

Still, an eruption of average strength can make ten times more noise than a jet airplane flying very low. But some large explosions, like that of Mount St. Helens, make only a light rumble. The noise is sometimes muffled by the ash. This and the heavy atmosphere surrounding the volcano keep the noise low.

This map shows the distance to which Krakatoa's explosions were heard. It also marks the areas in which ashfall was heavy.

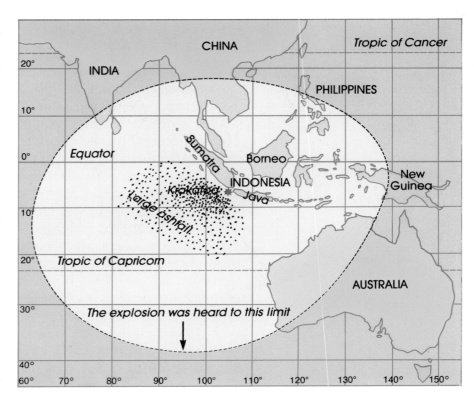

Can an eruption be stopped?

In 1973, lava flows from the volcano Helgafell threatened the island of Heimaey. The people used pumps and pipes filled with sea water to hose down the lava. It was one of the most spectacular and successful attempts to fight a lava flow. The Icelanders' efforts saved both their town and their harbor.

People have never tried to stop a volcanic eruption, for example, by plugging the crater. But they have struggled many times against the destructive force of volcanoes.

This struggle began as early as 1669 on Mount Etna in Sicily. There, a flow threatened the town of Catania. Peasants tried to detour the flow by digging a trench at its edges. The attempt failed. In 1983, another lava flow threatened a village. The experiment was tried again. But this time, they used dynamite to open the edge of the flow. Bulldozers then built huge dams to channel the lava. Still it did not work very well.

In Hawaii another plan was tried. In 1935 and again in 1942, bombs were dropped on threatening flows. This slowed the lava's speed.

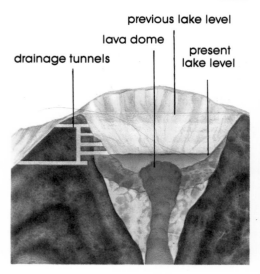

In the 1920s, tunnels were dug in the crater walls of Kelut Volcano. This drained most of the water from the crater lake and prevented overflowing. This is the only instance in which people have mastered a volcano.

In 1973 in Iceland, lava flows from Helgafell buried dozens of houses in a town on Heimaey Island. To save the town and its harbor from total destruction, rescuers tried something different. With hoses and pipes, water was pumped into the lava. The people hoped to cool the lava enough for it to harden. The pumping continued week after week. Finally, in June, the eruption stopped. The effort was a success.

During its eruptions, the crater lake of Kelut Volcano in Indonesia often overflowed. Each time, its flow of hot water, rock, and other matter killed many people. To prevent new disasters, the Indonesians drilled tunnels into the crater's walls. This was done to drain the lake and hopefully prevent more overflowing. With the tunnels, Kelut's crater has been held at a safe level for many years.

The beneficial flow

In January, 1973, a fissure erupted on the flank of Helgafell Volcano on Heimaey Island, Iceland. The eruption happened just 492 feet (150 m) from a nearby town. The island's population was evacuated. In three weeks, a large lava flow buried 350 houses. The eruption stopped in June, and the people returned to Heimaey. Five months later, the people decided to use the volcano's heat. They drilled holes into the thick flow. Next they pumped cold water into the lava. The water was later drawn out after it had been heated by the lava. In this way, the people of Heimaey could cheaply heat their homes. This method is used even today.

Can people cause eruptions?

People can cause volcanic eruptions. It has happened three times, on a small scale. None of the eruptions, however, were started on purpose.

One eruption took place in 1919 at Popocatepetl Volcano in Mexico. The volcano was being mined for sulphur. When dynamite was used to enlarge the mine, the crater collapsed. A fissure opened in the bottom. Thick lava oozed out, burying the mines.

The second eruption happened in 1941 on Mount Vesuvius in Italy. It was caused by an American bomber pilot trying to get rid of his last two bombs. The pilot threw them into Vesuvius' crater. The two explosions opened fissures in the dormant volcano.

Finally, in 1977, Icelanders accidentally caused a lava flow. They had been drilling near the Krafla Volcano, gathering hot steam. Magma rose through one of the holes the crews had drilled. The hole worked much the same as a chimney. Lava spurted from the volcano in the middle of the night. The drilling site was seriously damaged. This is the smallest known eruption.

Popocatepetl in Mexico is called "the smoking mountain." It was already of interest to the Spanish conquistador, Hernán Cortès, in the sixteenth century. He sent part of his army there to gather sulphur from the crater. The conquistadors used sulphur in their gun powder.

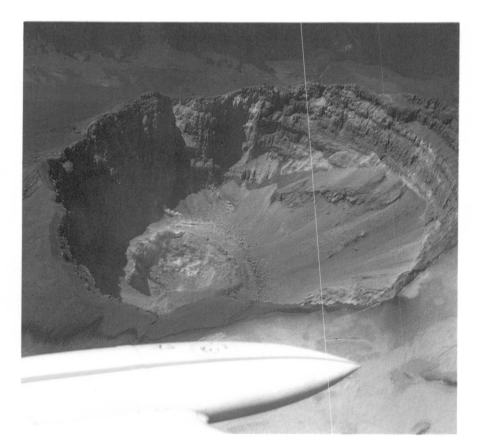

What should you do if a volcano erupts close to where you live?

Above all, do not panic. If possible, flee far from the erupting volcano. Sometimes volcanoes spew a lot of dust and ash. If this is true, take shelter in a solid building or in a car. But be careful. The layer of ash piling up on the shelter can reach a thickness of several inches. Its weight can cause the roof to collapse. So it is important to clean roofs often.

Avoid swallowing and breathing dust or gases. You can protect your mouth and nose with a wet handkerchief. A gas or dust mask is better if you have one. Some very deadly volcanic gases are heavier than air. These, like carbon dioxide, often gather in basements. It is best not to go into them.

Volcanic dust can quickly pollute rivers and kill plants. It is very important to have reserves of drinkable water and food.

Listening to the radio or watching the television can be a good idea. These will give you up-to-date information about the eruption. But avoid the telephone. You don't want to tie up lines that rescue services may need.

Lava flows, mud rivers, and avalanches of ash flow through valleys, just like the rivers do. So never stay in a low area. Climb to a high point to stay out of the reach of the lava flows. Watching a lava flow from close up is dangerous. You can be trapped.

Finally, if the erupting volcano is near the ocean, stay away from the beach. A tidal wave is always possible.

The eruption of El Chichon in April, 1982, covered everything with ash. It collected in thick layers on rooftops of houses and buildings in nearby villages. After the eruptions, the people cleaned the ash from the roofs of their homes. This was not done for the churches and other public buildings. These were abandoned. Their roofs eventually fell under the great weight.

What is the job of a volcanologist?

Volcanologists spend much of their time watching the volcano. They try to learn as much about it as they can. This helps them know when a volcano is likely to erupt. Then they can warn people and possibly protect them from danger. But to do this, the volcanologist must study every detail of the volcano. The cones, the domes, and the craters are examined with many instruments. These instruments send their reports to the observatory. The observatory is the volcanologist's work place.

To gather information, the volcanologist puts instruments called seismographs all around the volcano. Seismographs record any shaking of the earth. With other instruments, the volcanologist measures changes in the volcano's shape. Collapses, rises, falls, or movements of any kind are important. The temperature of the volcano's gases and lava is also taken regularly. This can be a very dangerous part of the job. Sometimes the volcanologist must go to the bottom of an active crater. There, gases are collected in tubes or studied on the spot.

To these measurements, the volcanologist must add other facts. These facts are gathered through research. Things such as the volcano's age, its lava type, the location of its fissures, and its history are all important. After that the volcanologists must decide what it all means. Even then, there is more work to do. Gases and rocks must be studied. Maps must be drawn. In the end, the volcanologist's work will lead to some valuable conclusions. From them, people will learn even more about volcanoes.

Being a volcanologist is a very interesting job. For certain, it is full of surprises. But it takes a lot of patience, cleverness, and much scientific study.

This orange instrument is a laser geodometer. It measures distance very accurately. Its measurements are usually not more than 0.0394 of an inch (1 millimeter) off per mile (km). The geodometer uses a laser beam to measure. The beam is bounced off a target on the volcano's side and returned. This allows the instrument to "see" change in the volcano's shape. It records even the slightest change. Here it is used on Mount Pelée in Martinique.

Do volcanologists know when a volcano is going to erupt?

Before a volcano erupts, it shakes, swells, heats up, and spits gases.

First the magma rises to the surface. There it fills the fissures, opening them with a series of jolts. Next it crushes the rocks. This may cause small earthquakes. These quakes often warn of a coming eruption. The quakes usually occur several days in advance.

Today, there are many ways to predict eruptions

1. Laser geodometer to measure expansion, or dilations, of the volcano.
2. Gas analyzer to record changes in the make-up of the volcanic gases.
3. Leveling to record changes in elevation.
4. Tiltmeter to record changes in the slope, or tilt, of the ground.
5. Seismograph to measure vibrations in the earth.

They tell people when an eruption is going to happen. Using this method, volcanologists on Réunion Island predicted an eruption at Piton de la Fournaise. They were able to warn people of it eleven days before it happened. They even knew exactly where the lava flow would begin.

In December, 1982, another volcanologist predicted an eruption on Mount Etna in Sicily. His warning was based on a series of deep earthquakes. This type of earthquake often happens before certain types of eruptions. The volcanologist said

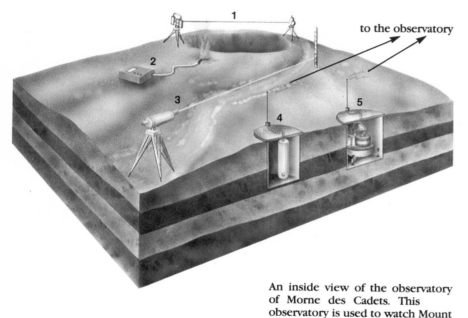

An inside view of the observatory of Morne des Cadets. This observatory is used to watch Mount Pelée.

Mount Etna would erupt in the last days of March, 1983. An eruption began on March 28.

As magma moves toward the surface, it fills fissures. It takes more and more room with each rise. This movement lifts and stretches the volcano. It is a little like the way a cake swells in the oven. These movements can be measured with sensitive instruments. In the past, volcanologists have predicted eruptions because of this swelling. A change in the volcano's size also marks the end of an eruption. As the volcano erupts, the magma that had swelled it pours out. The volcano deflates and collapses as its supply is used.

Often, as the magma rises, the volcano's temperature does, too. Thermometers and other instruments constantly watch the temperatures of the ground and the gases. They record these changes at the surface long before the eruption.

Finally, the amount of steam also increases as the heat does. This can be detected by the gas analyzer. This instrument measures changes in the make-up of the volcano's gases. Such changes were noticed at Mount St. Helens in 1980. The volcanologists predicted the volcano's eruptions hours before they happened.

Fifteen volcanoes now have these observatories. Since they were built, thirty eruptions have been predicted. But this is only a small number of the world's volcanoes. Many of the world's dangerous volcanoes do not have observatories. But these volcanoes can still be watched. Instruments that work automatically can be placed on these volcanoes. Automatic instruments send their information to satellites. The satellites then pass it on to observatories found far from the spot.

How do volcanologists protect themselves?

There are three dangers for the volcanologist who works on an active volcano. These are: gases, heat, and falling ash and lava bombs.

To breathe, the volcanologist wears a mask. The mask covers the person's mouth and nose. Its filter catches part of the dangerous volcanic gases. Sometimes the air becomes too thin. Then the volcanologist puts on a mask connected to an air tank. The tank is filled with oxygen. The volcanologist will use the air tank while working in a crater.

Volcanologists must also be protected from the heat of the lava flow. Each wears a fire resistant suit. These suits are covered by a coat of polished aluminum. This thin metal coat reflects eighty percent of the lava's heat. It reflects heat just like a mirror reflects the sunlight.

The volcanologist also wears a hood. It is made of the same material as the suit. It has a window in front made of many layers of glass. Heat resistant gloves and thick mountain shoes are also used. Dressed like this, the volcanologist can get very close to the lava flows.

Volcanologists must sometimes approach an exploding crater. They then use anti-shock helmets to protect their heads from falling bombs. These helmets are made of fiberglass. They prevent the skull and the

The volcanologist's suit is made of fire resistant fabric. It is also covered with polished aluminum. This metal reflects eighty percent of the lava's heat. In 1983, Maurice Krafft wore such a suit to work on Mount Etna. With it, he was able to work less than 3 feet (1 m) from the very hot lava. At times, the lava's temperature was 2,012°F (1,000°C).

neck from any shocks which might break the spine.

Most of the time, the volcanologist wears only part of this equipment. The weight of the oxygen mask, the suit, and the helmet slows the volcanologist. In an emergency, it may make fleeing impossible.

Has anyone gone down into a crater?

Volcanologists often go down into the craters. They plant instruments there or listen to the volcano. Most of the time it is quite routine. However, some trips are very dangerous. Some of them are very famous.

In 1934, two journalists were lowered into Mihara Yama Volcano in Japan. They wore fire resistant suits and gas masks. An enclosed cage carried them 1,365 feet (416 m) into the crater. Unfortunately, they had to turn back before they reached the bottom. When the volcano began to explode, the cage swung violently. The journalists were forced to give up.

No one has beaten this record for depth. In 1959, three volcanologists were lowered into Nyiragongo's crater. When they reached the lava lake, they had gone 1,312 feet (400 m). This

Two volcanologists used ropes to go into an active crater on Bromo Volcano, Indonesia. This crater is sacred. Once a year, the local people throw offerings into it. Their gifts include: flowers, money, chickens, and food. They are meant to quiet the gods who live there.

was fifty-three feet short of the record. Some people think that the chimneys in the crater bottoms are hollow. They think that these can be used to reach the volcano's depths. This is not true. Hardened lava usually plugs the chimneys only a few feet from the surface.

Can volcanic heat be collected and used?

A volcano's hot water and steam is a valuable source of energy. It can heat houses and provide electricity. It is inexpensive. Best of all, its supply is endless. This type of energy is called geothermal energy. Thirteen countries now use this type of energy.

In Iceland, 160,000 people use this source to heat their homes. One hundred drilling sites pump natural hot water from the volcanoes. Some of the water comes from great depths.

The oldest geothermal station in the world is found in Italy. There, drilling sites gather vapor at 392°F (200°C) from above a chamber of warm magma. This vapor is under a lot of pressure. The people use it to power engines that produce electricity. Eighty percent of the electricity needed for central Italy's trains is made this way. The geysers in California are used in the same way. They supply electricity to all of San Francisco.

Scientists are now trying to take heat directly from the magma chambers. Some tests have been done on the Kilauea Volcano in Hawaii. Kilauea's lava lake was in the process of cooling. At the site, a drill hit magma at 164 feet (50 m) below the surface. The magma's temperature was 1,922°F (1,050°C). The experiment was a success. But a good method of piping the heat out of the volcano has not yet been found.

Some day, a good method will be found. When it is, many countries will use this energy. There are many magma reserves in the western United States. Many of them are less than 6 miles (10 km) below the surface. These alone could produce more than enough electricity to take care of the whole country. They pump hot water from underground sources in the Parisian Basin and the Aquitain Basin. This method successfully heats over fifteen thousand homes.

The town of Beppu is a fashionable Japanese thermal resort. Vapor spouts forth from everywhere. Natural hot water is used here for many things. It is used in houses, swimming pools, greenhouses, alligator farms, local cooking, natural parks, etc. This water is simply rain water which has soaked into the ground. There it is heated. Later it gushes forth at a boiling temperature. Some of it comes from natural springs. Some of it is gathered by drilling.

Are volcanoes useful?

Indonesia has a hot and humid climate. Its soil is the most fertile in the world. This is because it is volcanic. Its volcanic ash is rich in minerals. Each eruption sprinkles the ash over the surrounding area. This natural and free fertilizer falls from the sky! The more often a volcano erupts, the more often the ash falls. And each time, the soil becomes even more fertile.

Volcanoes are actually more useful than harmful. They support the lives of 300 million people throughout the world. Their eruptions cause an average of five hundred deaths a year.

Volcanic earth is very fertile. This is especially true in countries where the climate is hot and humid. The ash from the eruptions is very fertile. This natural fertilizer falls free from the sky. In Indonesia, farmers gather three rice harvests a year because of this fallen ash! It is not surprising that some Indonesians have created a cult around their volcanoes. They consider the volcanoes the homes of generous gods.

Obviously, a very large ashfall kills the plants and crops. But if the layer is not too thick, new plants soon appear everywhere. However, a huge lava flow is a danger. In that case, the plants need more time, often dozens of years, to grow again. Despite the many eruptions, many people live near volcanoes. Because the soil is so fertile, it provides for many peo-

ple. Volcanoes are also good for another thing: tourism. Volcanoes in Japan, in the Hawaiian Islands, in Auvergne, and in Italy are visited by millions of tourists each year. They also visit the sites of many geysers, such as those of Yellowstone Park. People are fascinated by the beauty and mystery of these places. Their curiosity brings many benefits to those living in the area.

Even volcanic stones are useful. Whole towns in places like Mexico, Peru, and the French Massif Central are built with lava blocks. Even today, many walls are made with a mixture of volcanic cinder and cement. This mix makes the lightest, most insulating, and most soundproof materials.

And what about the huge amounts of minerals stored in old volcanoes? Tin, gold, silver, and diamonds are all found there.

Some craters eventually turn into lakes. These are a source of an excellent drinking water. Still others act like huge strainers. The ash in them filters the water, making it pure. Finally, others offer hot, mineral springs. These volcanoes make excellent sites for thermal resorts.

Volcanic blocks and bombs are a danger to volcanologists. To protect themselves, they often wear fiberglass helmets. These helmets rest on their shoulders. Their heads and necks are covered in case of a blow.

How can you become a volcanologist?

Volcanology, or the study of volcanoes, is an interesting field of study. Books and movies about volcanoes interest many people. Unfortunately, there is not much room in the field. It is difficult to make a career of it.

A student of volcanology might begin by visiting dormant volcanoes, like those of the Massif Central in France. Next, the person should go to see active craters. Mount Stromboli and Mount Etna in Sicily are good examples. There the flows can be seen up close. The student can smell the volcanic gases and see the ash and blocks in the sky. Being near

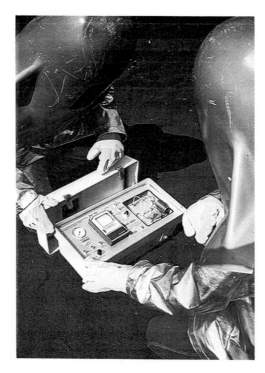

Volcanologists sometimes work in dangerous conditions. Their fire resistant suits protect them from heat and falling rocks. Here, they use an instrument which tests gases.

Seismographs are very exact and sensitive instruments. They can record the slightest ground movements.

an active volcano is a real test.

But to get into volcanology, a student needs more than an interest in it. It takes long years of study in high school, college, and even after. To this, a volcanologist must also add experience. This comes very slowly and may take years. But then very few volcanologists are tops in the field before twenty-five or thirty years of age.

A volcanologist's job can be fascinating. But it also has some risks. About 250 volcanologists work regularly on active volcanoes throughout the world. Several have been killed. As recently as May 1980, two volcanologists died on the job. They were killed by the explosion of Mount St. Helens in the United States. They were later found 6 miles (10 km) away from the volcano.

The Most Deadly Eruptions

Year	Volcano	Country	Number of victims	Cause of death
1815	Tambora	Indonesia	92,000	Famine caused by ashfall and glowing clouds
1883	Krakatoa	Indonesia	36,400	Tidal wave
1902	Mount Pelée	Martinque	28,000	Glowing clouds
1792	Unzen	Japan	15,200	Mount St. Helens type avalanche and a tidal wave
1783	Laki	Iceland	10,520	Famine following ashfall and gases
1586	Kelut	Indonesia	5,100	Lava flows
1902	Santa Maria	Guatemala	6,000	Ashfall and glowing clouds
1919	Kelut	Indonesia	5,100	Flows of hot mud caused by overflow of the crater lake
1822	Galunggung	Indonesia	4,000	Glowing clouds
1631	Vesuvius	Italy	4,000	Ashfall and glowing clouds
1672	Merapi	Indonesia	3,000	Glowing clouds
1711	Awu	Indonesia	3,000	Glowing clouds
1772	Papandajan	Indonesia	2,960	Mount St. Helens type avalanche and glowing clouds
1951	Lamington	Papua, New Guinea	2,940	Glowing clouds

In 1980, Mount St. Helens, in Washington state, erupted. It poured fire and ash over the countryside, killing many people and damaging billions of dollars worth of property.

Glossary

aa flow   a thick, sticky lava flow which often cools into rough, jagged sheets of rock.

basalt   dark gray or black rock. Lava, volcano craters, and the moon are all made out of basalt.

caldera   a pit at the top of a volcano that is more than one mile across. If a caldera is less than a mile across, it is called a crater.

carapace   a hard cover on lava that forms when water cools the lava.

chimney   the passageway in a volcano through which magma rises in order to get to the surface.

collapsed eruption   an eruption caused by the sudden emptying of a volcano's reservoir. This causes the volcano's summit to collapse.

core   the center of the earth.

crater   the pit that is formed near the top portion of a volcano. Craters are about one mile across. If a crater is more than a mile across, it is called a caldera.

crust   the outer part of the earth. The crust extends from the surface to about 40 miles (64 km) down.

eruption   in a volcano, the rapid release of gases, which causes the explosions that throw lava from the volcano.

fissural eruption   a less violent type of volcanic eruption. This eruption begins as a large crack in the earth. Very fluid lava gushes out along these fissures and runs in a path several miles long.

fissure   a narrow crack or opening, as in a rock face.

fumarole   a hole in or near a volcano from which gases escape.

geodometer   an instrument that gives extremely accurate measurements of distances.

geothermal energy   energy that is created by hot water or steam that is stored in the earth.

geyser   underground water springs that erupt from time to time.

Hawaiian eruptions   the least violent type of volcanic eruption. In this type of eruption, the lava is very fluid and flows quietly from several vents.

lapilli   one form of lava that is ejected from a volcano. *Lapilli,* which means "little stones" in Italian, can reach the size of tennis balls.

lava   a volcano's magma that has escaped to the earth's surface.

magma   the molten rock and other materials that are in the reservoir inside a volcano.

mantle   the part of the earth that is between the crust and the core.

meteor   a piece of matter that is floating in the solar system. A meteor becomes visible when it enters the earth's atmosphere.

meteorite   a meteor that has landed on earth.

plates   the twelve large pieces into which the earth's crust is broken.

obsidian   a shiny, black or banded volcanic glass.

pahoehoe flow   a very fluid type of lava flow. Pahoehoe flows move quickly and harden into smooth, folded sheets.

Peléean eruption   the most violent of volcanic eruptions. This eruption happens when gas builds up great pressure in thick magma. The pressure causes terrible explosions, glowing clouds, and hot ash.

pumice   a light, porous volcanic rock.

reservoir   the part of a volcano, deep below the surface, where the magma is stored.

scoriae   rough particles of burnt, crust-like lava. Scoriae forms when lava becomes very full of gas bubbles.

seismograph   an instrument that records shaking in the earth.

solfatara a term referring to volcanic areas that are rich in sulphur. The term originates in Italian and means "sulphur mine."

Strombolian eruption an eruption caused by gas escaping from a volcano's magma. In this type of eruption, the lava is often thick, causing violent explosions.

tidal wave giant waves in the sea. Tidal waves are often caused by volcanic eruptions.

volcanic ash particles of lava that are very much like sand.

volcanic bomb a large piece of lava, also called volcanic block.

volcanic block a large piece of lava, also called volcanic bomb.

volcanic dust very fine particles of lava. Volcanic dust is about as fine as flour.

volcanic form the part of a volcano that can be seen above ground.

volcanic rock lava that has cooled and hardened.

volcanologist a scientist that studies volcanoes.

volcanology the study of volcanoes.

Vulcanian eruption a type of eruption that occurs when magma blocks the central vent. This eruption has powerful explosions of ash and rock.

INDEX